Polly and Pete Make Masks

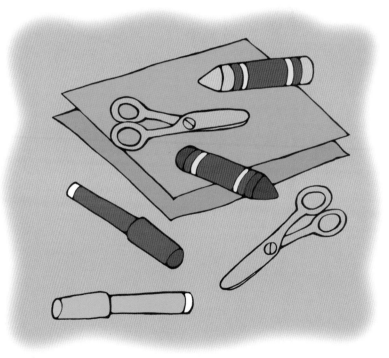

Dominie Press, Inc.

Peter Pig made one circle.

Polly Pig made one circle.

Peter Pig made two eyes,
two ears, one nose,
and one mouth.

Polly Pig made two eyes,
two ears, one nose,
and one mouth.

Peter Pig made one mask.
Peter Pig cut out his mask.

Polly Pig made one mask.
Polly Pig cut out her mask.

"I'm a dog," said Peter Pig.
"Bow, wow, wow!"

"I'm a cat," said Polly Pig.
"Meow, meow, meow!"